Fifty Ways to Achieve Excellence in Education

Building Student Relationships and Creating Success

PRISTINE
PRESS AND MEDIA

Dr. Jerry Darryl Thurston Wilson Lamb

Fifty Ways to Achieve Excellence in Education
Copyright © 2025 by Dr. Jerry Darryl Thurston Wilson Lamb

ISBN
978-1-969642-00-5 (Paperback)
978-1-964804-99-6 (eBook)
978-1-969642-01-2 (Hardcover)

TABLE OF CONTENTS

ACKNOWLEDGMENTS

The greatest gift that any human can give to another is life. To give birth to a child is something; to raise and educate a child is everything! We all exist for a reason, and we must not undermine the value of what it is that we have to offer. I am one man who sees himself as a beautiful creation that has the power to create. As a member of humanity, I know that I am neither greater than nor less than, neither focal nor separate from the very people who I share this world with. It is in this spirit of love that I write this book.

First, I would like to give thanks to God for using me as an instrument through which many needs have been, are being, and will be met. Secondly, I would like to thank my mother for her unconditional love and support and my son (godson) Sean, who I know this book will inspire. He has allowed me to stay focused, knowing that all good intentions and commitment have a life-altering ending. Third, I would like to thank my friends, in particular Jamie Cousins, Arben Mehmetaj, Debra Lithcott, Uncle Ralph Johnson, and Dr. John Jenkins, for their advice, guidance, and intangible support, which have allowed this book to come to fruition.

I would like to dedicate this book to my mother, father, grandmother, and grandfather, who have passed away. Without their love, discipline, high expectation, and principled guidance none of this would have been possible.

ABOUT THE AUTHOR

I would like to dedicate this book to my mother, father, grandmotherDr. Jerry D. Lamb earned his B.A. and M.A. degree in Criminal Justice from John Jay College in New York, M.A. in Special Education, Evaluation and Assessment from Hunter College in New York, M.S. in Administration and Supervision from Bernard Baruch College in New York, and Ed. D. in Organizational Leadership from Nova Southeastern University in Florida. He has been an educator for over twenty-five years and has taught on every grade level and educational setting. Early on, during his teaching experience at an elementary school in Harlem, New York, he came to realize the significance of personalized student relationships in helping students to succeed. This realization came to Dr. Lamb when he was operating his classes in a very military, regimented way but ran into several students who would not conform, no matter how decisive and relentless he was. Dr. Lamb observed how each student would retreat into his or her own world of drawing or singing or looking at pictures when experiencing confrontation.

Since Dr. Lamb was the president of The Golden Pyramid Fraternity, he decided to put together a mentoring program, in which students were paired with mentors who had similar interests and hobbies. The results of the paired relationships were immediate and absolutely astounding. Not only did the attitude of the students change, but so did their performance in class and at home. The parents, teachers, and students were so excited about this new experience, and life was better for everyone involved. It was only because of personalized relationships that these students succeeded. We know that they succeeded, because out of this small group, at least one-quarter of these students were the first in their families to graduate from college. Dr. Lamb still continues to mentor and develop mentoring programs.

Dr. Lamb is currently an educational consultant. He facilitates meetings of individuals and organizations on how to be effective educators through building meaningful working relationships with students. He readily admits that this is a challenging process, but he insists that it is an invaluable tool that educators need to practice if they are to fulfill their professional and personal legacy.

INTRODUCTION

Effective instruction begins with effective relationships, and this is particularly true in respect to educators who work with students coming from different cultural backgrounds. While there are a great number of programs that will instruct you on how to effectively teach, few share good ways to connect, motivate, and inspire students to succeed regardless of the various personal and societal challenges that they might face. This book will introduce a series of ways to open the doors of dialogue and connection, which is the basis from which students begin to believe in others and then in themselves.

You will discover that many students, in order to be inspired by you, have to believe and trust in you first. Once they feel that you can be trusted as their leader, they will empower you to become an effective leader. In return, you can empower them to believe in themselves by creating an environment that trains the mind to be constructive and optimistic. For you, success must be a mindset, because the mind is the tool that each student will have to exercise to engineer and navigate his or her life. Your role must be that of an architect, in which you help each student design a blueprint of success. This process can be a considerably lengthy journey and a formidable task. This is, however, what leading educators will face if they are committed to positively affecting the lives of children and indirectly, the community and the world, one student at a time! Make no mistake about it, one person can make a difference and as an educator you are in the unique position to become a great person of influence. Are you ready?

THE FIRST ELEMENT

The Philosophy and Principles of Education

From the time we are born, we are learning. The process of learning occurs through our senses, such as touch, smell, sight, and taste. Our interactive experiences allow us to interpret different events in different ways because of our varied perceptions. What we need to understand most of all about education is that it is, in fact, progressive in nature and requires that we evolve while experiencing both joy and pain. While some of us praise and encourage students to seek higher learning in the academic institutions of colleges and universities, there is another group that desires to seek learning in the trades and skills that require a mastery of vision and alternative solutions to problematic situations. Education is academic, and trade can be formal or informal. Whichever path students choose, one thing is of consequence, will the students you teach evolve to be responsible citizens in the community in which they live?

Educating students is very difficult; however, most educators are in this field because this is what they are destined to do. Educators must sometimes learn to put aside the egotism that tends to exist because of earned credentials. As an educator, you cannot have the mindset that you know it all or that students *choose* to fail. Education means that failure doesn't exist. This means that educators must be structured, yet flexible and creative enough to ensure that students absorb whatever information is being taught. The educator must be skillful in instructing students. If a student does not learn through a particular method, then another method must be utilized. When a student is not successful with a particular assessment tool, then one of two things must occur: Either the student must be instructed differently or the method of assessment must be varied. The sole purpose is to discover if a student has learned specified information. Student learning must drive collaborative instructional methodology and teacher approach.

Educators are lead learners and must learn to know the students with whom they are working. This is traditionally known as *teaching*. You will have to adapt and adjust your methods and style in order to educate students. It is your multifunctional adaptation to each student that makes you an effective lead learner. In fact, this process of learning how to address the needs of different students makes you a strategic educator. Trial and error are certainly the most effective ways to learn what works for different students. This is what makes you an educator for life; therefore, remember never to give up on your quest to learn and grow, to do so would lead you down a road of resentment, frustration, and burnout.

Vision and Mechanics

Popular leaders throughout history have all had visions. They have had great dreams and aspirations of the world developing into a place that their mind imagines. Not all great leaders, however, are popular or well-known. Therefore, what makes a great leader great? Without a doubt, it is a leader's ability to be both a visionary power and mechanical doer. While you yourself may not be mechanically inclined, knowing the details of how to do what you need to do, you will surround yourself with people who will construct what you have envisioned. Educators, by nature, are mechanical. You know how to do what you have to do. The next step is to be a visionary educator, who sees the intellectual creation of learning. This helps students to see themselves not only as they are, but for what they can become. At the same time, great leaders must exercise the type of vision that does not accept failure or see final destinations. If you have the vision of a great educator, you will create a system of natural leadership in which students will see themselves as a vital part of society, with a critical contribution to make. Understand that visionary educators who exercise the mechanics of *empowering students to learn* demonstrate the core of education. Just how grand is the world that exists in the small space of your classroom? Do your students transcend the space of their classrooms by expressing and doing things that make them happy, challenge their limitations, and heighten their curiosity?

Natural Curiosity

Young children have a natural curiosity. This natural curiosity makes it possible for them to learn more than one language at the same time and to have no limits to what they think and believe. As a matter of fact, their innate curiosity has no boundaries. You become a great educator when you are curious about the students you will teach and work with. Curiosity is a powerful intellectual driver for educators, because it opens you up to learning as you teach. Curiosity allows you to discover aspects and qualities about each student. When you learn something that is important to each student, you have established a clear pathway to connecting with them. You don't have to know anything about that one thing that each of your students loves, but you must be open to listening and learning. Once you are open, you will discover that students will share and teach you something that has valued meaning to them. The more they share with you, the more you become of value to them. Remember, in your personal life you only share information with those whom you trust and like. The more you share, the more valued that person becomes, that same rule applies with students sharing with you. Develop the intellectual curiosity that will lead you to the pathways on which each child walks. In doing so you will be more than a good educator, you will be a great teacher!

Learning is Naturally Uneven

One concept that educators must understand as they walk into the teaching profession is that students do not learn at the same pace, on the same level, or at the same time. Once this concept is understood, the skill of the educator is now called into demand, because you, the educator, will have to adapt and adjust your ability to identify and meet the needs of students individually. How in the world is this possible? Well, there are several ways to meet the needs of individual students. First, you must recognize each student's strength, and after you do, you will use that approach to assess his understanding of material being taught. For example, a student might be a poor writer but be very articulate and able to express ideas verbally. You should strongly consider having that student verbally demonstrate his knowledge of the information being assessed. That is not to say that you should not work on the student's written skills, but it *is* to say that learning is the objective of education. While it is true that all students can learn, they cannot all demonstrate in the same manner the knowledge that they have learned.

When you have a student in your class at a specific grade level, there is the expectation that at the end of the year that student should have acquired specific curriculum-based knowledge. This is not always the case, particularly in urban areas, where the classrooms are overcrowded, or in special education classes where learning disabilities greatly fluctuate. This does not necessarily mean that you have failed in your responsibility as an educator; instead, what it might mean metaphorically is that the plant will not be blossoming that season. Never think that you have failed as an educator if you have connected with, instructed, and assessed students in different modalities. In time, when the season is right, the information that you have shared with students will be demonstrated.

When you instruct students, you should have them work in a variety of ways, such as alone, in pairs, in triads, and in teams. You should also administer tests this way you will find it very interesting to discover that students learning from their peers can be extremely effective, because students are communicating with their peers in a manner that they can relate to and understand. Also, being assessed in these ways allows students to showcase their strengths while demonstrating their knowledge of information. You should also use movies or videos, CDs, computers, and smart-board technologies to instruct and assess students. There is no such thing as too many ways of instructing and assessing students. From projects to presentations, you will have covered all of the basic fundamental approaches to fully instructing and assessing students, and you will have earned the title *educator*.

SECOND ELEMENT

Systemic Approach

There are certain things that make students feel comfortable and one of them is an educator who is consistent. While it is extremely educational to be flexible and creative, it is equally important to have a method to the madness or just to be structured. Students like to know not only *what* is expected of them but also *when* it is expected of them. Having a standard system of how things function in class is important, because it not only helps to keep students focused, but it also allows them to develop a level of self-discipline. Students cannot use excuses when there is a system in place. There is a time for everything, and it is your responsibility to be structured enough to detail the flow of activities, yet creative enough to allow students opportunities to collaborate and work in a multifaceted way.

When it comes to being a teacher in a classroom, you must understand that you have to take on two roles, that of a structured leader with clearly defined boundaries, and that of educator which requires that you be flexible, particularly since individuals learn at different paces and on different levels.

Being structured is very important for a leader; it means that you have a system in place that allows you to effectively and efficiently operate regardless of the conditions of your environment. It also provides the reliability that students need as they take risks to achieve the high expectations that you demand. You should not underestimate peer pressure, and therefore, your ability to help students feel secure in stepping out of the group in your class means that they will be exposing themselves to a great deal of peer-subjected consequences.

Flexibility is necessary as well for a structured person. While a structured person will often have a strong desire to keep things at a specified pace, it is equally important to know and understand that, metaphorically speaking, grass does not grow evenly. There are some who will learn faster than others and others who will have more challenges than most. The difference is made by the leader's handling of the situations that may arise among individual students. You must focus emphasis on the fact that the main goal is to learn if a student is unsuccessful in one format or method of being assessed, another approach will be exercised in order to ensure that they learn. In other words, there are indeed "many ways to reach the capitol!"

Classroom Management

Classroom management starts off with the firm high expectation of the educator. The implementation of strong classroom management starts with the way in which a teacher presents himself physically, from dress to grooming. Believe it or not, it matters—perception is not necessarily everything, but it is notable. Another approach to setting the tone in your classroom is to stand at the entrance of your door and greet each student. I won't say with a smile, because depending on your environment, you may need to have a serious face. By greeting each student you are taking the first step in creating the need for communication. The next step is for you to introduce yourself and then establish rules of how every student is expected to operate in the classroom.

Leave the rules short. Some examples are, "Don't tease or put down another student," "Don't talk when someone else is talking," etc. The objective is to establish respect for one another in the classroom. Another (and extremely powerful) way to quickly establish classroom management is one I learned from my eighth-grade English teacher. It is to establish "rules of writing" for the submission of class work and assignments. Students act out and become unruly when they feel they have leeway to do so. If you teach a subject that involves writing, you should present your students with guidelines, such as the following:

- Write your complete heading on your first page.
- Stay within the left and right margins.
- Leave the last two lines of the paper blank.
- Leave the back of each paper blank.
- Start each sentence with a capitol letter, and end it with punctuation.
- Put a single straight line through any error, and rewrite the word beside it.

Once you have about twenty points on how assignments should be presented, give students a document to copy to ensure that they understand what is expected. By detailing how assignments must be submitted, you are removing the *leeway* mindset. When students do not follow the rules of writing, you must circle or identify where they made mistakes and have them rewrite the assignments over again and again and again, until they get them right, there is no leeway. In many cases, this could be a two to three day assignment, because you will not accept a paper that does not meet the expectations of presentation that you set forth. *You must* set the tone and not accept papers even if they have only one error if they don't follow the rules. You want to make it clear to your students that they don't even want to be in the grey or leeway area, in which they think they might get away with things. If you pay attention to the small things, very soon your students will realize that you are a detail person who pays attention to every little thing! Therefore, why would they try to get away with something because they will get caught!

This process is very long and tedious, and it will take approximately two to four months for students to fully adapt. However, once students adapt, your ability to teach and for them to learn will dramatically increase. They will know what is expected of them and that it is better to do it right the first time than to repeat an assignment ten times! This exactness of doing what you request is not limited to assignments, it also applies to students following your instructions and respecting your word. After about four to five months of exactness you can relax the exactness demand, because you want students to be comfortable. Everything has limits, and once you have set the tone, you need to ease up no student likes a pain!

The Power of Perception

"Perception is everything!" We have all heard this saying before, and while perception is *not* actually everything, it is very important. On the first day of classes, or in various situations, you can rest assured that not only are your supervisors watching and judging your actions, but more importantly, so are your students. I say that your students' impressions are more important, because your students are the ones who will have to perform in order for you to be considered an effective educator. Make no mistake about it! The way you talk, walk, interact, dress and even your facial expressions are all important. You are always on display and constantly being watched and interpreted to determine what type of person you are. You should always be authentic in who you are and what you say; nobody likes a phony, and students are quick to discover a fraud. In addition, be aware of any actions you display that might be misinterpreted. If you have a habit that might give off the wrong impression, you will need to make a conscious effort to adjust that type of behavior, while being true to yourself. As a passionate person, I always focus on people's eyes when I am talking to them, and while this is a good thing, I was unaware that I made facial expressions that observers said displayed a "You'd better do this, or else …" expression. Certainly, that was not my intention, and I became more aware and learned to relax my facial muscles when talking with passion. Passion is a good thing, and you need it as an educator, because it comes from the depth of your beliefs and convictions. There will come a time when you are tested. You might deal with a crisis or a situation that challenges your authority, just remember to put your ego aside and express the right emotion (calm and collected is not always the answer). Passion is good, because it allows students to feel and experience the depth of your seriousness but be in control of that emotion.

The Four *A*'s

Students are people, and as such, they judge their lead educator on the first *A*, which is *appearance*. The way in which a teacher dresses may seem somewhat irrelevant, but it can be used as a powerful tool of expression and modeling. Show that you care about your dress, even if you don't wear a suit. Overall, how much you know and how you treat others are significantly more important than how you might choose to dress. How you wear what you wear is what is really important, it's about style. Style is your personality expressed through walk, talk, movement, and dress. You have a great opportunity to display to students the various ways they can dress differently and express their individual personality without appearing inappropriate. As the lead educator, recognize that the ones you are leading do not have the credentials or the reputation that you have. Therefore, they need to be aware that they will be judged first on their appearance. If students are aware of this, they can use this insightful information to their advantage when interacting with people. In other words, if they can have a strong influence on how they are perceived before they even open their mouths, they have effectively set the tone of the initial interaction.

The second *A* is *articulation*. Students need to understand that they will also be judged on their ability to articulate themselves. One's ability to articulate thoughts and ideas is an essential part of effective communication. Students can be given examples of articulate and inarticulate speech via videos or role-playing. When a person speaks in a clear, firm, and concise manner, others will be able to understand what is being said. While it is acceptable for students to speak slang in their subgroups and in informal peer relations, you must emphasis that only Standard English is acceptable in communicating with you. Most students love to say that they know how to "speak good" (not *well*, but *good*). This, of course, is a clear indication that students need to not only practice articulating their words but also to know proper usage. The educator must encourage students to select someone they know who speaks well and have them emulate that person. Explain to them that it is completely acceptable for them to adapt someone else's style of speaking as their own, until they have discovered their own style in which they feel comfortable. Emulation allows the students not only to learn how to speak Standard English but also how to build a strong vocabulary base and intonation style, which will add emotional depth to what they say. They will resist in the beginning (and some will resist throughout the school year), but be relentless. Remember, *you only speak and understand Standard English.* The third *A* is *attitude*. Many successful people believe that life is 90 percent attitude (your response), rather than what actually happens to you. When you work with students, you know that they tend to be very impulsive and for the most part, pessimistic. They tend to look more at the negatives, the possible failures or cons of something, than at the positive aspects. This mindset is a defense mechanism designed to prevent them from taking risks, because nobody wants to fail or feel bad.

Do pessimistic people look at their capabilities from a strong and positive perspective? Do optimistic people look at their capabilities from a weak and negative perspective? What about you, are you optimistic or pessimistic? How do you view your capabilities? We can all agree that having a positive attitude is enormously important in being determined, resilient, and successful. If we can all agree on this fact, your challenge then becomes promoting an optimistic mindset in students that results in them responding to situations from a positive perspective. You can help students understand that many events happen for a reason, and it is those events that make them better people. It is not an easy process and often requires you to share a personal story, while you connect a series of seemingly independent events into a series of little events that have a meaning in the end. If you want to change students' attitudes, than you will need to changer yours. For example, if a student gets a problem wrong, you could say, "Almost, not quite." If a student says, "I give up," you should say, "That's not an option!" Remember, students will follow leaders who are strong in their convictions and push them to the next level of their own potential.

The fourth *A* is *action*. What people appreciate is effort but what people respect are results. As an educator you must be a *do*er, and you must likewise expect your students to perform at a level more advanced than what they believe they can and above what you anticipate. The power in action is in doing, not *trying*, but *doing*, because *to try* means "not doing." Try to clap your hands. Either you did or you didn't. You have to condition your students' minds that to do their best is, in fact, "doing." Even if things did not work out the way they planned, or they failed (as most like to say), this does not mean that they did not *do*. On-the-contrary, what it does mean is that they *did* put forth the effort (action); things just didn't work out this time. Remember, you should *always* put limits on what others consider failure. When a student says, "I can't figure it out," you correct them and say, "I can't figure it out *right now*." You never want your students to use the language that is pessimistic and limiting. The more you say something and then back up with action, the more students will respond to your words. If you exercise this fourth *A*, you will soon discover that students, as well as others, for that matter, will begin to act in a manner based on your words. Teach your students to demonstrate and earn this form of respect and empowerment.

THIRD ELEMENT

A Fork in the Road

Some educators believe that life is a sum of the choices that we make and the experiences therein. Whatever the case may be, once you are an educator there is no fork in the road. As soon as you have chosen the field of education, your aspirations should be nothing less than to help educate and inspire young minds. While not every educator keeps the same type of feeling that they had when they first decided to teach, the mission must still remain the same. You must constantly reiterate to your students that they only have to make one monumental decision in their lives. That decision is whether to choose a path of productivity and success or choose a road of pain and failure. Once this monumental decision is made, every smaller decision thereafter must be in support of the path that they have taken. In other words, every act should support the students' own predetermined destinies! If students feel that they can determine their own outcomes in their personal lives, despite the trials and tribulations that most humans experience, then they can maintain the mindset that, "No matter what happens, I will survive, I will achieve, and success is mine!"

Practical Solutions, not Consistent Complaints

There are many different ways to solve a problem, but there is one way not to, and that is to constantly complain. Complaining is contrary to the nature of an educator. As an educator, you are an explorer and a problem solver, and just as you encourage their students to find solutions to challenges that they face, you must heed your own advice. Whatever challenges you face when working with students, it is important to be very practical in your solutions. Solutions should typically be solved in stages. You will need to establish a simple goal that you would like them to achieve (with your support). This simple goal should be the first step in a series of steps toward conquering a particular challenge.

Preaching means very little without a strategic plan of addressing the issue. Typically speaking, whatever challenge you are facing with a particular student did not develop over a short period of time; hence, it will take twice as much time (in many cases even longer) to rectify. While it is true that you may not be able to solve a challenge with a particular student during your tenure, you certainly can do your part and exercise your wisdom as the student moves forward in life through your classroom. When you find yourself complaining about something, you should be providing a solution at the same time. From this point on, for every complaint that you have you should have at least one solution.

Don't Call for Help, Unless …

One of the worst things that you can do is call for assistance in disciplining a student, unless the student is extremely disruptive, threatening violence, or has become violent. As an educator in a class, you must exercise every possible idea and strategy of dealing with difficult students. You must address the issues head-on, because this is a student who you are charged with educating. You do not have a robot in front of you, only a human, and you will need to be the type of empathic lead educator who can connect with students. No matter how far apart your worlds may seem, you must make a serious effort to connect with and educate all your students. If there is a need to hold detention, then you should do it and hold it for an hour and a half, so that students will know that you are serious. Students must respect you as an educator if you are to effectively teach them. It is not an easy task, and in some cases you might not achieve your objective, but you must make a valiant effort. When all else has failed, then you can speak to another teacher or support staff to see what they can do to facilitate a resolution, and if that fails, then you must contact an administrator. The goal is simple, address issues in your classroom and support services first, through school administration second, and the child's household third for serious, *not* trivial, matters.

Making Mistakes

Mistakes are part of every great educator's journey in the pursuit of knowledge and understanding. You are the best type of educator if you are not afraid to privately and where appropriate, publicly admit your mistakes. Doing this once in a while (not too often) is not a sign of weakness, but quite the contrary, is a sign that you are secure enough in yourself to demonstrate that making mistakes is human. When you take time out to share with others an error that you made and hold yourself accountable, it empowers others to also demonstrate integrity. Addressing an issue means facing it and moving on, not having it come back up again and again or become a subtle question that lingers in the background to worry you. Any future references to your making a mistake and admitting it should be used in the context of "strong integrity." Similarly, when students make mistakes, it is important that you indicate to them that it is an important part of the learning process and that they should be commended for admitting them.

Students must know that all of the wonderful innovations that came to fruition were the result of trial and error. Once they understand that this is a natural and progressive function of learning, you can explore their mistakes with them, using this as a platform for learning. This evaluative process engages students in a critical thinking process. You want to make the subject of mistakes as exciting as solving a crime! You want students to engage in asking questions and following the reasoning process that will yield certain results. Furthermore, students' ability to accept the fact that they will make mistakes will encourage them to become risk-takers who are the explorers of the unknown and the seekers of knowledge.

Discretionary Power

Different educators operate in different ways. Some educators operate by the book and therefore any violation or small infraction is immediately written up and processed. Rules, policies, and procedures exist for a reason. That reason is to ensure the safety and well-being of the students and staff. As an educator, you will encounter many different circumstances in which students will cross the line and when this happens, the power of discretion must be exercised. There are clear cases in which the procedures must be followed. For example, if a student comes to school with a weapon or physically punches a student and causes bodily harm but most cases are not this clear-cut.

Students will be students, and they will often act in a way that is unintentionally reckless and thoughtless. When a student has crossed the line, you must seize this as an opportunity to walk the student through the possibilities of what could happen if you reported him. Let's look at a scenario where a student in class was flicking a lighter. The rules clearly state that students could not have lighters in school. There are two ways to handle this situation. The first way could be to report the student, in which case the lighter would be confiscated and the student would be written up and suspended.

The second way could be for you to confiscate the lighter and engage the student in a conversation as to why he had it. If the student had the lighter because he smoked, you can then relate a personal experience about the hazards of smoking or engage the class in a group discussion. The point is that you, as an educator, are *often* presented with meaningful opportunities to turn a punitive consequence into a learning experience. In addition, you must indicate to the student the consequences of his actions and inform him that should this ever occur again, you would report him, and the consequences would be administered and recorded in his files.

Discretion is a powerful skill that is designed to do two things, bring people together and provide the workshop for teaching and learning on a personal level. Personal lessons are superior lessons, because they are the direct result of a student's actions, as opposed to a history lesson, which lacks personal experience. When it comes to discretion, you, the educator, should know the student and have a feel for whether or not he would be responsive to your actions. My personal belief is that the most powerful lessons ever taught and learned will not be found in the textbooks of the classrooms, but in the personal discussions that take place in between formal learning.

Handling Multiple Needs

No teacher can handle every student's needs at the same time, all of the time with that said, it is true that every teacher can handle every student's needs some of the time. One thing that will allow you to be effective at addressing the needs of every student is to recognize when you are needed. While every student has a need, there are times when each student has a personal need that is so great that he demands attention. The demand for attention can be out loud or in silent isolation. The educator must know the pulse of each student. The *pulse* refers to typical behavior patterns. As an educator, when you determine a change in the pulse of a student, that is when you must recognize that there is a need for your intervention and assistance. You are handling an atypical situation and multiple issues as they arise. This is not that frequent, but when it does arise, you need to be aware and effective in addressing the specific challenge the student is facing. You have everything to gain in doing so, because the student will accept you as an ally, and allies are not easily forgotten or betrayed!

FOURTH ELEMENT

A Latch, Cylinder, or Combination

All students are different, and an educator's ability to unlock the door and connect with them all is, in many cases, not an easy task. There are three basic types of locks that keep people from walking into others' lives: latch, cylinder, and combination. Students who have a latch-type security lock are easy to connect with. All these students require is that you treat them with respect and be easygoing. They don't demand anything and they are willing to accept you as you are. They will make the adjustments, because their nature is welcoming.

Students who are cylinders are more complex; you can't just walk in and connect with them. This group of students is weary and not welcoming. They are not open to conversation and proceed with caution at every interaction. They look for the intentions of the educator and the sincerity therein. As an educator you must clearly establish who you are and what you stand for. In other words, in teenager terms, you must be *real*! If you are consistent and fair, honest and straightforward, the students will either accept or reject you. In most cases they will accept you, but you are wondering, *when*? Once the trust and mutual respect have been established and the students have accepted who you are, they will allow you into their world. Without a doubt, some students will try to scare or fight you off their property, as you get closer to finding the key that will allow you into their world. Students tend to put up their defense mechanisms and resist some educators, typically because they are afraid of you seeing their faults. Even though none of us is perfect, as humans we generally don't want to expose our own weaknesses and faults.

You, as a key, may only fit into some cylinders, while there are a few other lead educators who are master keys. As an educator, you should know which cylinder locks you can open and which ones require an educator who is a master key to open them for you. You don't have to open the door in order to enter into a student's world. An educator who is a master key can open doors to students who you cannot easily connect with and allow you to accompany him in. He can introduce and validate you as a good person whom that student can trust and begin to develop a relationship with. An educator who is a master key is essential as a connector or bridge. Every group has a person who is a master key and connector and for every lock there is a key.

Once in a while there is a special person who is a locksmith. He knows how to open everything, especially combination locks. This is a very special person, who is extremely effective. He should never be underestimated in his ability to connect with and influence students. He should be used on every level to help other educators connect with students. He possesses the skills to effectively introduce another educator's style and personality traits that the students either haven't connected with or have challenges connecting with. As you know, a combination lock is not easy to open, because there are so many possibilities and quite often, just when you think you have got it figured out, you find it's still locked. Students who are combination locks require a great deal of attention and time. Most educators quickly give up on these students and frequently don't want to deal with them. These students are often nonresponsive or the extreme opposite, unpredictable and overbearing. There is only one type of educator who will effectively connect with this type of student and that is the educator who knows himself and is able to have an enormous amount of empathy for them. When empathy is experienced on the deepest levels of authenticity, the students and the educator become synchronized. The educator knows not only how the students are feeling from day to day and also knows how to approach and talk to them. He clearly understands that everything he does, and how it is done, will be interpreted by the students as being either positive or negative. The powerful aptitude that this type of skilled educator possesses as a combination locksmith is his ability to know and articulate the potential of the students and guide them toward achieving the success that they desire.

Treasure Hunting

Every student has a unique gift to offer to the world and educators are in a fortunate position to explore and discover the treasures of each student. Treasure hunting is not easy and in many cases seekers don't find the treasure that they are looking for but the fact still remains that it exists. The process of discovering treasures is a tedious one, in which you must pay attention to every detail along the way. Once you become aware that each daily step is critical to reaching an objective, then the quality of your instructions and experiences will be greater. Knowing that you are on a treasure hunt when working with students will ensure that you take on a holistic approach to student success. The reward of finding treasures is always priceless and it is appreciated by all those who value student success on many levels.

Story Time

It doesn't matter whether you are teaching elementary school or high school do not underestimate the power of stories. We all love stories, because they serve to motivate, inspire, educate, warn, and explain many aspects of life. Reading stories in class will help students to develop and maintain the creative imaginary mind that is needed to be complex thinkers. When you tell stories it allows students to understand you better as an educator. It makes you more personable, because you have shared a part of who you are with them. We tell our children stories before they go to bed; we tell stories to help them avoid making certain mistakes. Stories, whether personally told or seen in the movies, are a powerful tool. The most effective way to get the attention of your students is for you to engage them in some of your personal stories. In time they will be willing to share their personal stories with you. This exchanging of stories is the strongest form of trust that exists in the educational field because it leads to students talking to you about problems and challenges that they are facing. As an educator, you want students to share their problems and challenges with you because this means they are seeking assistance. Assistance mean helping, helping means improving and improving means overcoming. You may not feel qualified to advise a student about certain issues, but you are qualified to connect them with a person or service that will effectively address their needs.

A Sense of Humor

There is nothing like a good sense of humor. If you take time out to think about some of the people who you or others love to be around, you will discover a couple of things: either they give great advice or they have a wonderful sense of humor. A sense of humor means that you are not only happy with yourself as a person. It also means that you have a degree of flexibility in life that allows you to understand that not everything is guaranteed or works like clockwork. The ability to laugh at situations that might otherwise be daunting means that you are able to step back and take a look at the big picture. You might say to yourself, "It could be worse," or "Life goes on." Your ability to smile and let go will significantly reduce the amount of stress that comes with educating students.

In addition, a good sense of humor is one of the most effective ways of reducing the perception of insurmountable challenges that students face. If you are able to crack a joke or find humor in the midst of a situation that needs to be de-escalated, then you have demonstrated to the student that not everything is as bad as it appears. This feeling of being able to be happy, enjoy life, and accept occurrences in life will not only free the educator but also the student from the bonds of fatalism and hopelessness. Everything natural has a balance and therefore, while humor is effective, it should not be excessive. The next time you are stressed out, think of an incident that was funny. Replace that self-destructive energy with the flow of life energy, which does not get clogged up in repetitious negative thoughts. This not only applies to you but also your students. When you share with them some jokes or funny stories, you allow them to see you as a real person, with feelings and experiences that are real and which they could relate to. If you get a smile out of them, then your goal is complete. A smile, in every culture, means one, thing happiness.

A Touch of Class

Humans have some basic needs and one is the need to belong. The sense of belonging can be initiated by a simple handshake or the exchange of words. Asking how students are feeling or what's new or shaking a student's hand, means a great deal. Students appreciate educators who take time out to acknowledge and greet them. Think about how you would feel if somebody were to frequently greet you by your name in a pleasant manner. Handshakes between male teachers and male students are particularly meaningful and set the tone for a mature engagement, because there is a posture and firmness that comes along with a greeting between the two. When you pat a student on the shoulder and tell him that he is doing a good job, it will make him feel good about himself. One moment of encouraging contact between an educator and student will create the type of motivation that sometimes words cannot express.

Know Their Needs and Priorities

Most educators tend to exercise the concept that students, for the most part, are on similar levels. With this belief, there is the assumption that the household that students come from has caring parents who are able to provide for them. There isn't a single educator who wants to imagine students living in a shelter or a household in which the parents may be on drugs, don't care, are unemployed or don't feed their children. The fact is that there are many students who are faced with formidable social and emotional challenges. These are issues that they often find embarrassing and frustrating. Consequently, they do not share their feelings with anybody they keep them inside. This creates not only a ticking time bomb, but also the type of erosion that prevents students from focusing on daily academic activity.

Most educators would state that it is not their responsibility to address personal issues. However, if you are a master educator, there is no other option than to address all problems that you know exist and which affect your student's performance. As an educator, you need to know where each student is at emotionally and where his priorities are. When students are faced with serious social issues, such as their parents having no electricity in their house, then you should communicate to the social worker this issue that is affecting the family. In another situation, you might discover that a student is living with a grandparent who doesn't cook and therefore the student does not eat three square meals a day. You then can speak with the social worker or administrator to see that the student gets free breakfast and lunch in school. Your ability to identify the needs and priorities of your student is essential to your success as an educator. When you pay attention and address issues that arise, it allows students to develop a level of respect and appreciation that validates your authenticity as an educator.

Your Words Mean Everything

It is never a waste of time to talk with and motivate the students that you are responsible for educating. Talking is meaningful if you have something to say, otherwise, it is better to remain silent and observe. Everybody loves to hear positive words and productive advice. If you can offer words of encouragement, however small, while it may not make an immediate difference, it may very well be a seed planted for future reference. Words are indeed powerful and their effects can create success beyond your wildest imagination. However, when you talk with people, be sincere. Nobody wants to work with, listen to, or confide in anyone who is not sincere.

Talking to someone is much more empowering than most people think. Most people think that it is a simple exchange of words and ideas. I submit to you the idea that conversations and interactions are much more than what meets the eye. Let's view the power of conversations in the context of your influence. How do you know which students you influence? You might respond quickly by saying, "It's the ones who listen and follow your instructions." However, the fact is that your influence is not dependent upon *your* perception but rather the student's interpretation and weighted value of what you say and how you say it. Influence does not have to be continuous, it can be momentous. There is always a powerful and defining moment in a student's life. As an educator who constantly works with students, you have a higher probability of creating that momentous experience if you are sincere in your interactions and conversations. As life would have it, you might never know when you have forever altered the life of your student, or anyone, for that matter, with whom you have interacted. Therefore, be empathic and there will be little doubt that your influence and impact on others will be positive and long-lasting.

Feel What They Are Saying

A successful lead educator must be a good listener. While your primary responsibility is to educate others, if you are an effective lead educator you will know others you are working with and what some of their desires are. This is significant, because if you know what people desire and you help them to achieve their goals, you have just recruited the support of a determined person. How important is listening? It depends on who is talking! Listening is important to the speaker and only after a feeling of connection is established is it important to the listener. When educators listen to their students, what they are doing is receiving the trust of the students. When students talk more it means that they are willing to risk being wrong, being judged, or being looked at differently, etc. Therefore, when a student talks, what is being shown is the desire and effort to connect and trust the educator. Think about *feeling* in this respect, the more you feel what students are saying, the more you are trusted, valued, and can establish influence. Feeling is more than just listening, it is understanding the emotional process, it is empathy.

Every time you listen, not only do you gain knowledge and insight into who a student is, but also how they feel, think, and operate (their style). A lot of educators don't think that this information is important, because to some, teaching is generic. Effective educators know that neither teaching nor learning is generic. Once you become aware of this fact, then you will be more adept at creating a style of connecting and teaching that is receptive to the differences that each student has. The most efficient way to ensure that students advance while in school is not only to talk with them, but to listen to them.

FIFTH ELEMENT

Make Students Feel Special

Most students have a need to feel special. Feeling special means that they have connected to someone who makes them feel good, different, and meaningful. The very purpose of life is to be meaningful. When you have free time, tell a particular student who may need to be motivated that you are coming to one of their basketball or soccer games just to see them. When you do show up at the game, make sure that you are seen by that student. Give a high five or handshake and if they are far away, simply point to him. Let that student know that you didn't come for any reason but to see him, and when you see him in class, take time out to talk about his success, either out loud or in private, use your discretion. The amount of connection and empowerment you receive from the student is well worth the extra few hours after school. It's a worthy investment. For those students who do not play sports or engage in extracurricular activities, it may mean that you will have to discover their hobbies and either purchase magazines for them or simply have a discussion with them about their hobbies. Always strive to make those students that need the extra push or those that "fly under the radar" feel special. Your ability to go that extra mile means that you are one step closer to meeting the holistic needs of students in your class.

Let's Go for a Walk

Walking can have a great deal of content meaning and is often symbolic of a journey. Taking walks with certain students provides an opportunity for in-depth connection. *In-depth connection* is used to describe the symbolism of walking with the students on their journey, on their path to wherever it is that they are going. By physically walking with students, you indicate to them that you understand that they are traveling on their own paths and that you have the ability to both lead and empathize with them. This connection is qualitatively meaningful, because it is a one-on-one experience, which is personalized. Furthermore, the act of walking side by side is symbolic of partnership and connection. This physical adaptation of keeping the same pace is an agreement of sorts, because you both are doing the same thing at the same time. When you walk with a student, there is an understanding that your time together is limited. Therefore, the focus tends to be more intense and memorable. Make your moments of walking with certain students count. If your timing is right, it can produce meaningful lifelong effects that will help guide students in the right direction.

Three-Legged Race

There are some students who come to school and just go through the motions of what is required. When they are being academically or personally challenged, you will never know, because they will not openly express their feelings. These students tend to fly under the radar because they do not act out and their work tends to be average to poor, fluctuating up and down. Watch for these students in your class and your peers' classes, because in most cases, the way these students can most effectively succeed is through the three-legged race! The three-legged race means that you will have to connect with the students and let them know that you will partner up with them in order for them to experience success. It is understood that ups and downs are a joint venture and that achievement of a specific mission is uncompromising. Imagine this relationship as a literal three-legged race, in which you have to motivate your teammate. When they stop, you stop, and when they fall, you fall, but you quickly get up and demand the same from them in order to move forward. You both become tied together by the common concept of "we are one." Once students agree to have you as a partner in the three-legged race, the rewards for them will be great, and for you, greater because you know what could have been.

Mentor a Student

The power of mentoring is that it is a compassionate act that allows a student to grow while experiencing a level of support that is indeed rare. Being a mentor is a choice that both the mentor and the mentee have to make, because it is a partnership. If he is seriously committed to overcoming various challenges he may encounter, the mentee must be willing to trust and follow the mentor. There are different types of mentoring objectives, and each determines the duration of the mentoring relationship. Mentoring means that you are taking an interest in a particular student or students. It means that you are being a good listener and giving sound options to your mentee.

A mentor is a guide, whose tasks are to motivate, inspire, support, and educate their mentee on how to be successful, with a no excuse attitude! In some cases it is very demanding, but quite often it's about the mentor being available when the mentee needs help or guidance. Educators can be powerful mentors! While this is not an employment responsibility, educators should ask themselves the question, "If I am unable to mentor students, how can I effectively teach them?"

There are too many educators that have a complete disconnection from their students. It cannot be over emphasized that an educator's ability to connect with students will exponentially increase the impact that he or she will have. Mentoring can be formal or informal. During the course of your teaching, you will, if you are an effective educator, come across a student who either will choose you or to whom you will take a liking and want to mentor. You don't want your power to be in your *title* you want your power to be in your *influence*. Mentoring is one of the most effective ways of earning influence, not only with a particular student with whom you are working, but also with other students who are aware of your ability to be concerned and caring. If you are an educator in the middle or high school, in particular and you're not mentoring a student, then you will need to take a good look at whether or not you are "being your best"!

SIXTH ELEMENT

Dreams are for Everyone

When you ask elementary students what they would like to become when they get older, you will hear them cite many different professions. As time progresses, this variety of dreams slips away and if you were to ask high-school students what they wanted to become, you would discover that they either don't know or they are choosing a path that is common or stereotypical. In order to keep the dreams of possibilities alive, you must encourage students to think big. One way that you can do this is to display various pictures of wonderful things or places that exist in the world, which students can aspire to have or to experience. Another thing that you can do is to have students create a dream board showing what their lives would be like if they could wish it true. Everybody does certain things for a reason and if you can give students reason to have a strong drive, by finding their passions in life, then you will have discovered a fire in them which cannot be extinguished!

If you are a holistic lead educator, then your students' wishes will be fueled by their willpower and their dreams will one day turn into reality. Additionally, you could have students discuss what they would love to do and why. It is fair to say that some students might have dreams that are unrealistic, but if the dreams are the motivation that keeps them in school, then, indeed, their dreams are of great value. Find the students' passions and they will work with you!

Teach Something Not in the Books

Every once in a while you should teach something that is not in the books. There is nothing more fascinating than teaching and learning something that is different. Everyone likes to learn something new, particularly something that most people don't know about. When you take time out to teach something new, realize that it should *not* be something related to the subject that you are teaching instead, it should be something interesting or intriguing and maybe even something for which you, the educator, would not know the outcome. Let me make this absolutely clear, learning is not based on time, it is based on experience! Therefore, it doesn't matter how much time you spend, but it does matter that you are all participating in the activity. The best part of teaching something new is that in this activity you are only the teacher of one activity; the other lessons belong to the other students in your class. That's right, have your students teach you and others something that they have learned in their life experiences, from cooking to dancing. Everybody needs to teach something that is not in the books!

Win, Win, Win

There is nothing more rewarding than winning! Winning doesn't mean you have to be number one. It means that you have to achieve a level of success that meets certain expectations, goals or standards. When you are a leader, it is critical that you start off with a series of short-term wins. What this does for you is demonstrate your ability and effectiveness as a leader. Your success has to do with getting students to work with you in order to both maintain a flourishing environment and to help them improve their academic standings.

Another *win* is that of the students. You must create guaranteed wins for students, whereby a series of successes on given tasks can be earned weekly by following instructions, or doing well on tests, quizzes, or homework. You can also be creative in ways that allow students to be personally recognized for their neatness, punctuality, dress, positive attitude, and so forth. These series of successes will not only motivate your students to continue to do well— they will also create a developing level of self-esteem that will ensure that they become risk takers. This is essential, because as the level of challenges increases, students will have to work harder to achieve greater levels of success.

Finally, teamwork is what a lead educator must practice as the final steps in developing a unified vision of success. Both the lead educator and students must have joint successes, in which they are recognized for their collective achievements and partnership. While usually this type of *win* is dependent on outside recognition, the lead educator or key students can position themselves into situations where they can work together, be successful, and be recognized as a group. There is also the option of individual success which can be attributed to group effort and therefore leads to group recognition. It all ends up being a win-win-win situation!

Think Chess, Not Checkers

Chess is a very advanced game. It requires that each player not only thinks, "What if I did this?" but also, "How can I achieve a specific goal in the most efficient and effective way?" Creating a perception and establishing an environment of comfort are essential to achieving your goals. Therefore, design and decorate your classroom in the fashion and intensity that will move students toward your goal. This does require you to invest money in your classroom. It is a worthy investment, which will yield big payoffs in the end. You have to be personally committed to success, which means you will be required to go that extra mile. You don't have to, but I have never met an authentic educational leader who did not! In addition, you need to know which students should and should not sit together. If you know the pulse of your students and class, you will not only know *what* to do to avoid disruptions and optimize learning, but *when* to do it. Knowing what to do, when to do it, and how to do it all require advance planning. Think chess, not checkers!

Post Power Words

Words are powerful because they are one form of communication. The fact that we use them every day of our lives to convey messages, feelings, desires, and necessities means that they are important. Words are so powerful that different cultures and subcultures have traditionally created new words to describe the feelings and thoughts that a particular group feels. Words and feelings are connected. As an educator, you want your students to feel a certain way and quite often you might become frustrated. Students are not as mature as you would like them to be or do not think in a progressive way that will allow you to effectively teach them or so you think. Then you may come to the realization that students that have challenges might come from an environment in which the type of thinking that they are utilizing is necessary for them to function, fit in or survive. In order for you to create a new mindset, you will need to take simple, but powerful steps. Posting key words such as *resiliency, compassion, forgiveness, honesty*, etc. will allow students to visually take in meaningful words that exist in certain mindsets.

When you post words around the room, understand that they should be in areas where students constantly look, thereby ensuring that the message is being communicated effectively. Good places to post pictures can be right behind the teacher's desk, by the window, or at the top of the blackboard. If you watch where your students most commonly tend to look, you will have discovered the most effective place to post your words. Post no more than five different words around the room, unless your words are theme based, such as virtues. By displaying up to five words around the room multiple times, you allow the impact to be powerful, because it is the same small group of words seen over and over again. Things that are short, but repetitious, are easy to remember! That is why commercials are typically less than thirty seconds long and are played over and over again. Finally, you should frequently refer to the words that you display in your classroom. Simply displaying a word does have an impact, but when it is frequently used as a point of reference by the teacher a full connection will be established. It will not fade into the background, it will have value.

Technology is a Friend

There are many different ways that you should instruct students, as I stated earlier. Having students watch something on DVD to reinforce what you have instructed in class is an effective way to help students retain information. It also allows you to ensure that your class is not boring. Furthermore, you should encourage students to hand in assignments that are typed for extra credit, and do presentations in Power Point, overhead, video production or even through audio recordings. Try exciting activities that require the use of these technologies and you will not only entertain your class but bring the group closer together.

You and your students should bring in a song on CD that you really love and that makes you feel good about life. Sit around in a circle and have each student describe the song everyone is about to hear and tell why they love it. Watch what will happen! Another exciting activity can be to have students use a digital camera to capture images that demonstrate a lesson that was taught in class. In order to prepare students for the workforce that awaits them, take every opportunity to use technology to advance the learning process.

The Power of Delegation

Delegation is a powerful way to develop a meaningful, close relationship with students. Once you have an understanding of your students and their needs, there will come a time when you will need to empower certain students so you can address their needs. There are some students who are extremely hyperactive and with all that energy, there is only one thing that you can do to effectively ride the waves of their need to move around. You must give them tasks that will *require* them to move around. Likewise, you should give students who are creative the tasks of creating and designing your classroom. *Delegation* means that you are empowering someone. The objective in this act is to be the recipient of support from the students. You empower them and they in turn, empower you. As an educator, you have an authority and leadership role by the nature of your position. However, true power comes from influence!

Most students enjoy responsibility, especially when it is within their comfort zone. When students meet the expectation of their teacher to do certain things this builds a level of confidence and trust in the teacher. This type of relationship results in the students giving power to the teacher to determine what their potential is. This is an exciting stage because when the time comes for the students to move out of their comfort zone, that extra push and motivation by the teacher is all that is needed to move them into challenges that will help them develop. An educator who delegates responsibility demonstrates that not only does he have an abundance of power that he is willing to share, but also that he wants to receive the partnership and be empowered to improve the lives of the students he is working with.

SEVENTH ELEMENT

Success Is Mine and Yours

What does the word *success* really mean? For some, success is defined by a high score received in a classroom test or standard exam. For others, it is getting into the college of their dreams and yet for others, it is the pure accumulation of material trophies or money. Let's talk about what real success is and the impact that it has on all people involved in the experience. If you were to look at a child or a newborn baby, what three main things would you wish for him or her? Like most of you, I would wish for love, money and the best that life has to offer. While all three are very general, let's go through each because they all symbolize what you will contribute to the life of each student with whom you come into contact. Love is something that every human being needs and wants as part of being alive. Love is a feeling of belonging to something greater than just yourself.

Love is a powerful emotion, which brings, joy, happiness, and every feeling that makes one smile and another one cry. Love is freedom, it is peace, it is unconditional and without reservations. Love is what we have the choice to give because it is a part of who we are. Do you give love? Do you give a piece of *who you are* in the educational setting, expecting nothing in return other than gratitude that you had the opportunity to change someone's life for the better? We consider having money a sign of success, only because it provides *options*. Therefore, what we are really saying is that we wish students had the ability to choose what they want to do and be able to do it without fear! In other words, we want them to experience life fully! Are you living your life to the fullest? Are you alive? The best that life has to offer is only revealed when you explore, interact and learn about what exists in your world. Keep in mind that the best is designed to make you a better person and therefore, you will and must encounter the challenges of life that will build the character, convictions, resiliency, and compassion that you need to appreciate your life.

Have you experienced the best that life has to offer? Success is many things to many people however, what it must *not* be is something at the end of your life. Success is something that must occur along the way. You are the *educator*, the *lead learner*. You are the one who gives love, provides the options in life and introduces learning. You are the dream parents have for a newborn, the hope of the struggling child, the creator of the world that we live in. Too many educators have completely underestimated the power that exists within them to radically create a new earth. This can be done one student at a time by simply being what you ask of each student, a success. Along the way, not in the end, success will be as it is designed to be mine and yours.

Becoming Influential

There are different levels of effectiveness an educator can experience. The first is based on your position, the second is based on your likeability, the third is based on your consistency of action, and finally, the fourth is based on your actions and what you stand for. When you meet students for the first time, they know that you are the teacher and they are the students. The roles are clear and understandable and students will respond to you based on your position. This is what is expected, however, as an educator you should want to move to the highest level of influence. Likeability is valuable, remember, students will do almost anything for you if they like you.

Once you establish this connection however, you have a stronger responsibility as a lead educator, because students will hang off your every word and action. The power of being consistent in your actions demands a respect that many students admire because they understand the fundamentals and process by which you operate. They might not feel a strong personal connection, but they do not dislike you and therefore they will respect you.

The ultimate level of influence that you want to earn is that of being personable, respected for being fair and consistent. In the end you want to be remembered as having the ideals or the attitude that motivates and inspires students to think of possibilities and act on them. The reputation and aura of this type of leader is both transparent and transcendent. It allows him to be many things to many students and certain things to certain students. He is the one who knows which key will work and which combination will unlock the doors of student potential. His ability to reach this level lies in his skill in connecting with the needs, wants and ideals of students. This type of leader is authentic in nature and needs no script for expressing his words and actions. You should aspire to be this type of influential leader, which needs no title because he is a reflection of the best aspects of what exists!

You Are the One

Just so you know how special you are, I will tell you now that there is a student out there that can only connect with *you*. This student can only hear your voice and appreciate your story. This student can only feel what you feel and see what you see. You are the one who can lead him, teach him, and guide him to better lands. You are the path and the bridge, the scolder, and the healer. You are the one! By nature (which you may call coincidence) or by choice, because the student has chosen to allow you into his world, you are the one. As you are the one, other teachers, administrators, or the parent may seek your assistance in helping the student to move toward a better situation than they are currently in. You don't have to help a million people to be great just the ones with whom you come into contact and certainly, the ones that choose you to be "the one." To be selected in this role is an enormous privilege and you should be extremely grateful because the student has seen in you something so special, so beautiful, and so grand that he wants you to take part in the shaping of his life.

Fine Line

There are some educators who love their field of employment and they recognize their gift to connect with and help others. This gift can often become a burden, if the educator becomes too entrenched in the circumstances and challenges of particular students. There are many students who have some serious issues and it takes a special educator to help address these challenges. The challenge for the educator however, becomes how to balance the depth of commitment in helping a particular student. This is something that only the educator can determine, with the advice of other support staff and friends. In most cases, the educator is tackling social issues that must be addressed in order for the student to be successful on any level. While some educators may think that it is inappropriate for a particular educator to become deeply involved in helping a particular student, it is not, as long as the educator is not working in isolation. It is important that an educator work with the parent, psychologist, social worker, or any appropriate team, planning and addressing the needs of the student. In many cases the educator is the most powerful and influential person in the student's life, not only because the educator is physically there on a consistent basis, but also because educators tend to be more decisive in their feelings, thoughts, actions, and principles. The educator therefore becomes the leader of the team that will help a student, rather than being a secondary participant. A word of wisdom, to the advanced empathic educator, would be to follow your heart and conscience, and balance this with your limits and contributions. Everything should be balanced in order for things to be healthy and to function properly—the yin and yang.

Finding the Connector

You cannot always have a perfect connection with every student that you teach. While you are the lead educator and you are the enforcer of classroom rules and expectations, it is important to know when you are *not* the most effective person to meet the needs of a particular student. Having the ability to recognize when you are not the one is important, because it allows you to step back and find out who *is* the one. There is somebody out there with whom the particular student has already connected or has the potential to connect. You have to use your skills to find that person, the one who can act as an interpreter, mediator, and support system to effectively meet the needs of that student.

As much as your ego wants to be the be-all and end-all in every situation with every student, as a lead educator your role is to *facilitate* achievement. Your task is simply to ensure that your students achieve the highest possible level they are capable of, even if that means you have to enlist the support of others. Getting the support of others is not passing the buck, it's called strategic planning and it is the execution of a no-exception, no-excuse attitude of student success. You must never be so proud or controlling that you will not seek to use the skills and talents of others around you to help you achieve the goal of helping your students.

Weathering the Storm

The cyclical nature of life requires that there be ups and downs, good days and not-so-good days. You will encounter, particularly when starting out, some challenging times. On a storm scale of 1 to 10, I suggest that you prepare for a 9.5 and batten down the hatches! In the twenty-first century, a new type of educator is needed, one with a strong sense of self and a determination to create a paradigm shift in the mode of thinking and doing in the educational field. This type of educator must begin to build a structure that demands student self-control and the achievement of high expectations. The new type of educator required to create this shift must be strong, resilient, assertive, determined, structured, and fearless. There is a process that he must undergo to attain the level of commitment and skill set required to make this paradigm shift. The students of today are that challenge!

Students of today are very difficult! They have been empowered to do as they please and once they are challenged by an educator, it is the educator who is often called into question. It is not fair, but it is a reality that educators face, particularly in urban areas. The problems of the community and the household are literally carried over into the schools. Furthermore, since you, the educator, are not the parent of these children, you are limited in what you can do. You are put into a situation where you feel hopeless, but more importantly, powerless. This however, cannot be the attitude, particularly of the new educator. You are here to stay and you must weather the storm. What you have to offer is greater than the consequence of allowing students to be set free into a world in which they might be as reckless as they are currently. You must weather the storm because there will come a time when the clouds of despair will subside and the clashing waves of rebellion will ease. A ray of hopeful light will appear. No storm will last forever, but the scars of failure will!

Only One Degree More

The difference between hot water and steam is only one degree. Once you, the educator, understand that the break through to connecting with a student is similar to that one-degree difference, you will never give up. Educators are constantly telling students that they must never give up, and giving up is certainly never an option for parents. This is a mindset that dictates success at all costs, under any circumstances. While the students that you teach are not your biological children, they are your moral responsibility.

An educator is a lead learner and as such, must be open and aware of the possibilities to help a student succeed. When you tell a student to never give up, you must take heed of your own words. What you say to students you must yourself believe in and practice. Let me repeat this again in a more powerful way. *Are you a living example of what you are asking a student to become?* If you are, when you tell a student to never give up, then *you* will never give up. For you, that one degree is only one more step. If you believe in success, then it is important not to get caught up in a student successfully passing a test, but rather a student successfully living life. You will recognize that you are a contributing factor to that student's continued success that goes far beyond an academic test; you are the *one degree more* which adds meaning to their life.

There is an enormous amount of energy in going that extra mile and being that one degree. However, as an educator, you have the greatest powers ever given to humans. Just like the sun above, you have the power to scorch the earth or cause the lands to flourish. The power and ability to do both lies in your mindset and your will power! Think about life or sporting competition and you will discover that most people, not knowing how close they were to success, just gave up when they were only steps away from achieving their goals. This is true not only for the students, but also for the educator who gave up in the last hour because he believed success would not occur. Once you understand success, you will never again give up. You will always and without hesitation become the one degree more, and you will ensure not only that the student knows success, but also that you, the educator, will be complete in both your professional and moral responsibility.

Eighth Element

Art of Negotiation

Not everything should be accept or reject, yes or no. An educator's ability to teach students to negotiate is a powerful skill that is often not encouraged. When you demonstrate negotiation and allow students to negotiate something, you are, first and foremost, allowing them to be aware of the art of never giving up; second, finding common ground; and third, recognizing that they will have to learn how to look at the big picture. All educators have the mindset that students should never give up. Unfortunately, when students run into certain challenges, they are quick to say they give up if things don't work out the way they plan, or if they are confronted with a no! *No* is extreme in the sense that it means "not at all," but is this really what *no* means? Of course not! There are degrees of no. When you teach students to negotiate with you and others some of the time, it allows them to ensure that every rock of possibilities has been turned over. *"No"* only means "no" when all of the possibilities have been exhausted.

Second, teaching students to find common ground allows them to discover the needs, wants, and desires of others. Think about that! How powerful and skillful is it to discover and identify the needs of others? It is natural for people to look for and focus on their own needs, but it is simply awesome to be able to identify the needs of others and skillfully meet them on common ground. This is a principle of negotiation.

Lastly, helping students to identify, understand, and focus on the big picture is important. Students have things that are important to them and that they want. However, they often get caught up on the smaller things in life, which can dramatically take them off-course. For example, a student may want to move on to the next grade level, but keeps cutting English class because he doesn't like the teacher. The discomfort of disliking the teacher is small in comparison to the big picture of passing the class and moving on to the next grade level. It is important that all educators help students look at the big picture. When a student looks at the big picture, which means he has come to a major fork in the road. He has made the one decision that he needed to have made to begin walking on the path of success. If a student chooses success in life, then every decision thereafter should be made as a single step in that direction. The major fork in the road does not happen daily it only happens once. Certainly a student can pivot or change in the wrong direction, but the bottom line is that he only needs to make one choice and one decision, success or failure. Which did you choose? While no person is perfect, have you moved in a direction that will allow you to obtain your big-picture goal? The art of negotiation as articulated here is not about manipulation and deceit to get students what they want for their benefit only. It is the mutual ethical and moral standard of reaching an agreement.

Understand the Reasoning

In order to effectively help students to develop properly, you must put aside the mindset of "right" and "wrong," "agree" and "disagree." This type of mindset is an enormous obstacle in addressing the needs of students. How many times have you had an argument or discussion with someone and your position was that they were wrong, and you were right, or that you disagreed with them? How do you resolve your conflict or win your argument? On a daily basis, you work with students who might not agree with what you are teaching or the importance of that information. The way to resolve most conflict or address serious issues, for that matter, is to be *understanding*.

Understanding is a powerful force of analytical depth, because it has nothing to do with you agreeing or disagreeing. Instead, understanding has to do with your ability to gain insight into others' beliefs, perspectives, and most importantly, reasoning. The *reasoning* is the most important part in addressing issues or conflicts, because it represents the blue-print or path upon which a student has traveled to reach or establish their position. If you are able to understand this journey, then you will be able to more effective identify what misinterpretations have occurred, or what went wrong and when, etc. Nobody wants to be judged, particularly students. Their ego is so fragile that they do a lot of things simply to fit in rather than doing what is right. You have to be an understanding person first! If you maintain the mindset that you "disagree" with a student or that a student is "wrong" every time you interact with them, then you will have shut down your ability to listen. Then you will hear nothing and therefore, you will be able to do nothing meaningful to affect the lives of your students.

When students detect that you have made up your mind that they are wrong, they will automatically close their doors, because you have closed yours! If, however, you listen to their reasoning process and ask questions to gain a further understanding, and when appropriate, have them reflect on their actions, you allow them to reevaluate possible alternatives they could have exercised to bring about different results.

Don't Be Mean, Be Fair

Students will often label teachers as "good" or "mean." These labels say a lot about how students perceive the fairness of a teacher. A student can certainly have a very strict teacher and in the end label that teacher as being "cool," or "good," but "strict." A student could have had a very free-spirited teacher who he labeled as "mean" and "not strict." The difference is in how educators communicate and treat other students. Communication is an important part of being perceived as fair or not. If you warn students and you articulate your expectations multiple times, you are clearly openly letting every student know what you feel and why. No student can say that you did not on several occasions articulate your expectations, and the consequences for not abiding by standards. That is indisputable, even if they sound off in the class, saying, "No, you didn't say that." Remember, you don't need students to verbally agree with you. All you need to do is have a meeting of the minds, during which there is agreement of what is and is not appropriate, as established by classroom and school rules. *Fair* means that you have not only warned them, but in fact, you have given students an opportunity to work off consequences. By taking this approach, you have even further established your position and can unequivocally be acknowledged as a "fair" educator.

Give Them a Way Out

Don't we all want chances to improve, be forgiven, and do over again? While it is important that educators be structured and develop a system of operating, it is equally important that a student be given an opportunity to earn his way out of a tight spot. For example, if you give a student detention because he was talking or playing too much in class, you might say to him publicly or privately, both serve a different purpose—"If you behave today in class and do your work, I might consider taking you off of the detention list." You have now empowered him with the opportunity to earn his way out of detention. It is up to him, he has a way out! This opportunity granted to him allows other students to see that you are fair. It will demonstrate to them that not only are you a structured educator who implements consequences for undesired behavior, but that you are not so structured that you can't recognize that they are children. Students will consider you fair, because the choice of getting out of detention is theirs, not yours. Although students cannot always earn their way out of detention, they will clearly understand that they must demonstrate self-control if they want to avoid consequences.

You Will See Them Again

The responsibility of educating students is not only part of your professional choice. It should be part of your personal passion. In making it personal, you will create a level of connection and commitment that enlightens students far beyond the history lessons taught and math problems solved. When you take a personal approach to educating students, you develop a meaningful, in-depth level of authenticity, which students will appreciate throughout their lives. While you may not live in the same community as the students that you teach, you must work to develop the level of connection that a person in the community would have. In doing so, you are always ready to cross paths with your former students. This crossing of the paths in the future is particularly meaningful, because you are meeting outside of a school setting and in a place where you are not in an authoritative role. How the interaction takes place between you and the student says a great deal about your effectiveness and your authenticity as an educator.

Remember, as the educator, have the greatest ability to impact and influence students, in many cases even more so than their parents. Think about your personal life and the experiences that you had in school. How influential were your teachers in your life? If you educate students with the idea that they live in your neighborhood and you will see them and their families again, there certainly would be few questions about your concern for their future, because you have a personal investment.

NINTH ELEMENT

Act, Don't React

Regardless of the location and population of students that you are working with, you will discover that students will certainly test your patience. When they do test your patience, you will need to learn how to act and not react to the emotional rush that often follows after a student has challenged your authority or behaved in a disrespectful or unacceptable manner. When you become aware that a student has stepped out of character, take a deep breath and pause, because your ego will want to rush ahead and meet the challenge with a greater challenge. Once you have learned to pause, you will be able to look at the big picture and determine how you should respond to a situation in order to achieve the big-picture objective. If you have ever taken Tai Chi, Aikido, or Wing Chung martial arts, then you know that the most effective way to handle conflict is to yield to forceful energy and redirect it. Regardless of your gender, consider learning one of these three martial art styles, this is not only physically healthy, it is mentally healthy.

Time Management

There is only so much that you can do in one period, in one day, in a week, or a month. Effectively managing your time will allow you the opportunity to complete your lessons, keep students active, and have free time. Time management will also allow you the opportunity to map out how you intend to effectively educate students. Knowing that most students have short attention spans, as do adults, you might break up a fifty-minute period this way: five minutes to settle in and take attendance, ten for instruction, a twenty-five minute activity, five-minute summary, and five-minute explanation of homework questions and answers. Follow a format such as this, watch students pay more attention and see time fly for both you and the students.

Now let's look at the school week. Not every day should be the same, variation should be important to both the educator and the student. For example, if you teach English, then you might plan your week this way: Monday, bring in newspapers and discuss current events; Tuesday through Thursday, work on core curriculum lesson; and Friday, conduct review and group discussion of journal topics. This structure is extremely effective for students with short attention spans, who tend to get bored quickly. They like this structure, because they only have three days to get the information that they need for the core curriculum. Now, your monthly schedule would look something like this (you have a theme approach every month): one of the weeks may require research on material, another week you might be watching videos or reading books, etc., a third week would be for presentation, and the final week would be for evaluation. As an educator, you must be creative in your presentation of information, student activities, and assessment. If you are successful at time management, students will learn, time will move quickly, and you will have a very good school year!

Don't Charge by the Hour

You decided to be a teacher for a reason and that reason must always be at the forefront of the decisions that you make. Over time it becomes easy for educators to get fixed on the notion that they will not do anything unless they get paid hourly. While unions do exist, you must understand that this should not guide your passion to care and share. There is nothing wrong with the spirit of volunteering. It is the spirit of you going that extra mile that moves a student from poor standards to good and from good to great! Students are able to detect sincerity and authenticity. When you fail to participate in different events or to provide that extra hand, they will feel that you do not care. Is that perception worth that extra hour? If you love what you do, if you are concerned about where you teach, if you want to see the results of your influence, then you must become a part of the structure, the institution, of the school. Student success is primarily determined by a level of your commitment. No one is asking that you work for nothing, but you should be asking yourself why you are working in this field and why you have this *natural talent*.

The Ripple Effect

In the stillness of a pond, which would you choose to become: a rock, which causes ripples far and wide, scaring the fish and sinking to the bottom, or a piece of bread, which floats for a while, catching the attention of a few fish at first and a school thereafter, and never sinking to the bottom, because its purpose was fulfilled at first sight? There is power in any force of energy that you choose to become, but you must be aware of the effects of your action. With all of the intentions that you have, actions will be balanced out by the perception of the students. Therefore you must be authentic and work from a foundation in which you are always doing what you feel is in their best interest. In doing so, students will know you as good. Without a doubt, educators face many challenges and are often drained emotionally, but whether you are pedaling your bike or not, the wheels will continue to spin because of momentum. You must push forward, you must steady your energy from day to day, and you must be the effect that will attract the school of fish.

Take Care

You need to take care of yourself if you are to be the most effective educator that you can be. How important are you? Well, how important is a mechanic who fixes the engine, a detective who solves a case, a pilot who navigates an airplane, or a surgeon who saves a life? You are all these things and more, so you must make the time to care for yourself and your needs. Failure to do so will result in failure for others. The holistic care of yourself means that you will have to attend to your mental, emotional, physical, and spiritual needs. Once you have balance in your life, you will be able to help students to effectively balance scales in their lives.

Your mental health requires that you frequently take time out to pause when you feel that you are becoming frustrated. There is no need to become stressed, because stress serves no purpose other than to disorganize that which is stable. It will also help if you make a point to not take things so seriously. When you are able to look at the big picture and understand that in the end things will be okay, then you will be able not to take things so seriously. When you get upset, think of something that will make you feel better, think of a time that made you laugh. Thinking of good experiences will allow you to break your mind's tendency to replay an unpleasant experience over and over again.

Emotions are certainly powerful feelings that influence not only how you treat yourself but also others. Therefore, it is important to confront and address issues in your personal life that create emotional instability. It is not an easy task however; it is one that is worth addressing. One of the most effective ways of dealing with emotional issues is to acknowledge and accept that a particular situation exists. A second way is to develop the most effective plan to address the challenge that exists. A third way is to have a team, or at least one person, who will listen and give you sound motivational advice. Fourth, *stop* replaying the past experience over and over again, and *stop* thinking about what could happen in the future, because that is the *direct* result of your anxiety and emotional torment. Finally, make sure that you utilize your time in a fashion that will keep your spirits high. In other words, do what you know makes you feel good. You must strive to balance the scales of feeling bad with feeling good, when you start feeling down.

Many educators might very well believe that their personal health has little to do with effective instruction of students; this is simply not the case. All around the country there are educators who are frequently absent because they get sick or have a chronic medical problem. Then there are some educators who come to school but are lethargic, and constantly sit down, and don't interact with the students. If these two things alone don't significantly affect student learning, then you are correct in saying that a teacher's personal health doesn't really matter. I am quite sure that most people would, however, agree to the contrary! Therefore, here are some simple ways to improve your health. The first thing that you should do, early in the morning, is drink a twenty-ounce glass of water. Doing this in the morning will cleanse your body, line your stomach, and help provide the natural absorption needs of the human body. Make sure that you eat breakfast and take a liquid multivitamin by tablespoon in the morning. Enjoy healthy snacks at work and drink plenty of water. Needless to say, you should have a good lunch and dinner (not a late one), along with exercise. For those who are truly not motivated, walking around the block or up the stairs is good enough. All educators can agree on one thing students can drain all of the energy out of you! So take care of your heath, it really does matter.

Finally, spirituality is very personal and while it is not directly related to instruction, it does provide you with the sound foundation that you need in your life to feel and be complete. Your completeness and your need to have positive faith are important in your interactions with others. Therefore, exercise your spirituality in a manner that is comfortable and gives you the highest virtues and compassionate traits, which will allow you to be the best person that you can be. Your students' success is dependent upon your unyielding passion and commitment to help them learn and experience the best aspects of your education.

Conclusion

This book was designed to unlock the doors of your mind and the windows of your vision, so that you will truly be the great educator that you are. You are more influential than you will ever know, more caring than most will observe, and more talented than others can rate! Your success is forever linked to the success of your students and those whom you had the ability to influence. While there are unlimited numbers of books and workshops on how to instruct students, the last untapped variable that greatly affects student learning is an educator's ability to connect with and positively influence his or her students. With the seeds that have been planted in this book, you are on your way to being a more effective educator.

You can profoundly affect all you come into contact with by sharing with them who you are. You are the *x* and the *y*. You are the, *what if*'s and the *why not*'s. You are the *near* and the *far*. You are *kind and the good* because you help students to become *great*!

MOTIVATIONAL MOMENT

You Are More Than You Will Ever Know

In that one moment of silence at the end of the day, when you let out a sigh as your body begins to rest its weary self, remember who you are. You are more than most will ever know, and you are more than everything that you wished to be when you first started teaching. It is true that you may be tired or burnt out, but you are still alive. As long as you are alive, you, like your students, have the ability to rejuvenate the best of who you are. It is not easy, but it is not impossible. I ask you, *Who are you to give up?* What makes you so special is not that you provide the essential academic skills that allow students to be forever successful and enable them to move one step closer to achieving their desires. What makes you special is not that you provide the high expectations that demand the students be progressive irrespective of the social or conditional challenges that they face. However, what does make you special is your *authentic sincerity* to be a *servant* to the students, parents, community, and humanity at large. If you never thought of yourself as a servant, look again. What you do is provide the needs and wants of others on a constant basis. While some might look at being a servant in a negative light, I assure you that serving is not a negative thing. You serve a greater cause than most will ever come to know. You serve as the guide to curiosity and knowledge; you serve as the platform for determination and resiliency; you serve as the model for love in which each brick must be put into its proper place to ensure that every student can withstand the storms of life's challenges. *How great can any student become?* Better yet, how great can the leaders of the world be, if it were not for the quiet servants, the educators, laboring with the authenticity of their heads, hearts, and souls? It is *you*, the educator, who builds the spiraling steps toward the tower in which the great leaders become beacons of light that inspire and lead others. If you think for one minute that your affect only extends to the student who sits in front of you, then let me awaken you from your dream. Like a rock thrown into a still pond, your impact on the life of the student who sits before you ripples outward in his sphere of influence. You are more than you will ever come to know, and you are more valuable than the pearls of the ocean and diamonds of the river. You will come to witness this in the silent moments of life, when you are *still*. In those moments, you will capture the happiness of a student whose life you once touched. You will know then, at that moment, you are *good* because you did your best to make each student *great*!

RESOURCES

For more information on how you can build a learning organization that allows you to more effectively communicate with students, staff, administration, and parents, contact the *Thurston Wilson Organization*, to take advantage of one of the following available services:

- Motivational speaking
- Seminars and workshops
- Group coaching
- Consulting Services

Thurston Wilson Organization
www.ThurstonWilson.org
Contact@Thurstonwilson.org